THE MEADE FAMILY HISTORY

England to Connecticut

By

Katherine Fletcher

THE MEADE TREE

The Meade family was first found in Somerset since the early Kings of Britain.   The name might mean "meadow" or living around a meadow.

This particular Meade family came from England to Connecticut and were some of the first settlers in Greenwich, Connecticut.

MEADE FAMILY TREE

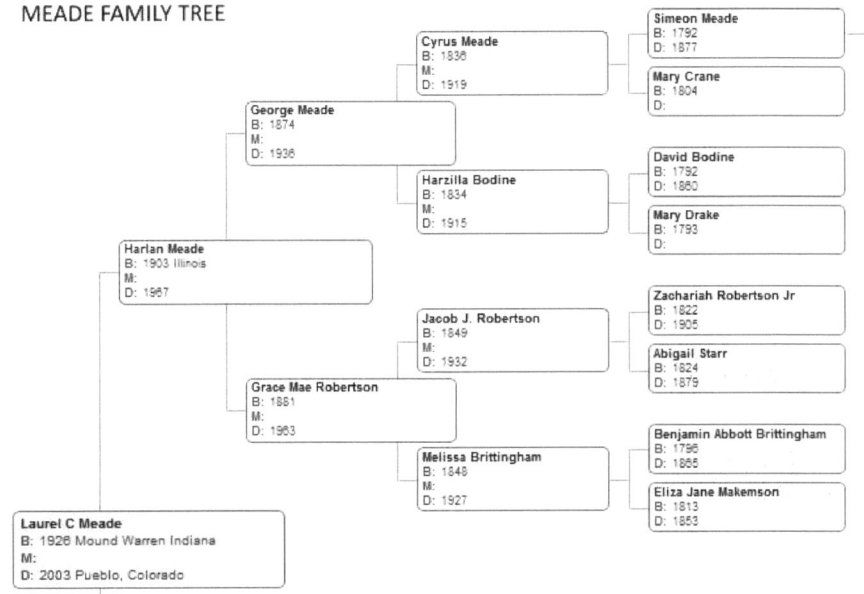

Here is the Meade Family continued more generations

MEADE FAMILY 2

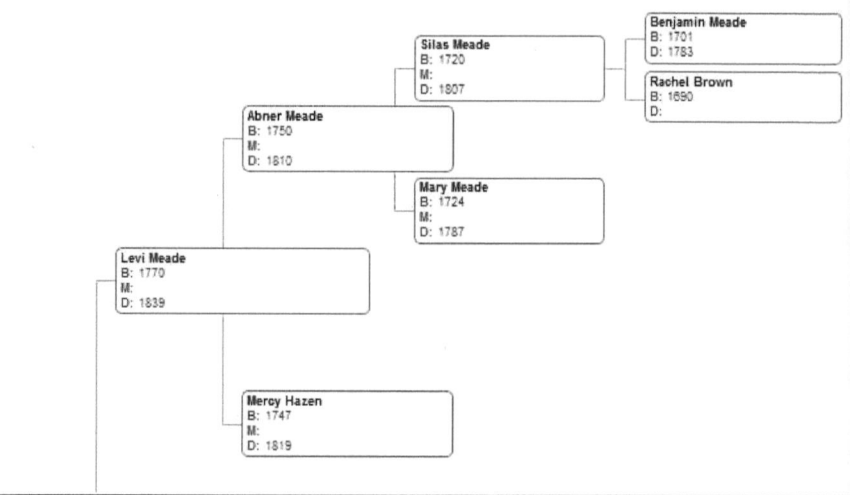

Benjamin Meade
B: 1701
D: 1783

Rachel Brown
B: 1690
D:

Silas Meade
B: 1720
M:
D: 1807

Mary Meade
B: 1724
M:
D: 1787

Abner Meade
B: 1750
M:
D: 1810

Levi Meade
B: 1770
M:
D: 1839

Mercy Hazen
B: 1747
M:
D: 1819

GENERATION ONE

LAUREL Clem MEADE and Margaret

Born 1926 in Mound, Warren Indiana. Died 2003 in Pueblo, Colorado

His brother is Byron Joe Meade. They live on a farm.

Here's his obituary:

Name of Deceased: Laurel C. Meade
Age at Death: 77
Death Date: 16 Nov 2003
Obituary Date: 20 Dec 2003
Newspaper Title: Commercial-News
Newspaper Location: Danville, IL, US
Birth Date: abt 1926
Locations Mentioned in Obituary: Perrysville, IN, IN Perrysville
IN, IN
CO, CO
Agriculture,
CA, CA
OH, OH
of Pueblo, CO, CO Pueblo
Pueblo, CO, CO Pueblo
West Lafayette, IN, IN West Lafayette
Rocky Ford, CO, CO Rocky Ford

HERE'S THE WORLD WAR II ENLISTMENT RECORD

Name: Laurel C Meade
Birth Year: 1926
Race: White, citizen (White)
Nativity State or Country: Indiana
State of Residence: Illinois
County or City: Vermilion

Enlistment Date: 10 Jun 1944
Enlistment State: Illinois

Enlistment City: Fort Sheridan
Branch: Air Corps
Branch Code: Air Corps
Grade: Private
Grade Code: Private
Term of Enlistment: Enlistment for the duration of the War or other emergency, plus six months, subject to the discretion of the President or otherwise according to law
Component: Reserves - exclusive of Regular Army Reserve and Officers of the Officers Reserve Corps on active duty under the Thomason Act (Officers and Enlisted Men -- O.R.C. and E.R.C., and Nurses-Reserve Status)
Source: Enlisted Reserve or Medical Administrative Corps (MAC) Officer

Education: 4 years of high school
Marital Status: Single, without dependents
Height: 00
Weight: 040

GENERATION TWO

Harlan J. Meade (1903) and Caroline Clem (1906).

born in Illinois and mother born in Indiana.

Birth: Oct. 11, 1902
Death: Jun. 1, 1967

Family links:

Parents:

George Meade (1874 - 1936)

Grace Mae Robertson Meade (1881 - 1963)

Sibling:

Harlan J Meade (1902 - 1967)
Robert C. Meade (1908 - 1950)*

Burial:

Spring Hill Cemetery and Mausoleum
Danville
Vermilion County
Illinois, USA

Caroline Clem's parents are Charles Clem (1868-) and Myrtle Stevens (1868-). Her grandparents are Abraham Clem (1826-1905) and Margaret Ann Taylor (1828-1900). Her great grandparents are Henry Clem (1788-1855) and Martha Carmichael (1788-1832). This "Klemm" family goes back to Ittlingen, Heidelberg, Baden-Wuerttemberg, Germany.

GENERATION THREE

George Meade (1874 - 1936) and Grace Mae Robertson Meade (1881 - 1963)

Birth: 1874
Death: 1936

Family links:

Parents:

Cyrus Mead (1836 - 1919)

Harzilla Bodine Mead (1834 - 1915)

Spouse:

Grace Mae Robertson Meade (1881 - 1963)

Children:

Harlan J Meade (1902 - 1967)*

Robert C. Meade (1908 - 1950)*

Siblings:

Edward E. Meade (1868 - 1949)*

Clara Bell Mead Lynch (1871 - 1933)*

George Meade (1874 - 1936)

GRACE ROBERTSON

Birth: Jul. 16, 1881
Death: 1963

Family links:

Parents:

 Jacob J Robertson (1849 - 1932)

mother: Melissa Brittingham (1848-1927)

Spouse:

 George Meade (1874 - 1936)*

Siblings:

Hallie Gertrude Robertson Stambaugh (1873 - 1899)*

Grace Mae Robertson Meade (1881 - 1963)

Faye M. Robertson Clem (1884 - 1968)*

 Grace's parents are Meslissa Brittingham (1848-1927) and Jacob J. Robertson (1849-1932). Her grandparents are Benjamin Brittingham (1796=1865)and Eliza Jane Makemson (1813-1853).

GENERATION FOUR

Cyrus Mead (1836-1919) and Harzilla Bodine Mead (1834-1915)

Birth: Oct., 1836
Death: Apr. 6, 1919
Arrived in America in 1855 at age 19 and in 1860 lived in Vermilion, IL

I believe he fought in the Civil War on the Union Side from NY.

Family links:

Spouse:

Harzilla Bodine Mead (1834 - 1915)*

Children:

Edward E. Meade (1868 - 1949)*
Clara Bell Mead Lynch (1871 - 1933)*
George Meade (1874 - 1936)*

Burial:

Spring Hill Cemetery and Mausoleum

Harzilla Bodine's parents are David Bodine (1792-1860) and Mary Drake (1793)

GENERATION FIVE

Simeon Meade (1792 Connecticut to 1866 Vermilion ILL) and Mary Crane (1805-1870)

Birth: Jan. 23, 1792 in Connecticut
Death: Feb. 11, 1877
Vermilion County
Illinois, USA
Son of Levi & Mary Ann (Ferris) Meade; headstone has Mead not Meade.
 Family links:

Spouse:

 Mary Crane Mead (1805 - 1866)*

Children:
 Anseleny?? MEAD 1826 –
Hulda Ann MEADE 1829 – 1907
Levi MEAD 1832 –
Stephen Decatur MEAD 1833 – 1846
 Esther MEAD 1835 – 1846
Cyrus MEAD 1836 – 1919
Lucinda MEAD 1838 – 1846

Mary Frances MEAD 1842 – 1856
Charles MEAD 1842 –
Mary MEAD 1845 –
George MEAD 1847 –

GENERATION SIX

Levi Meade (1770-1839) and Mary Ann Ferris (1768-1839)

Levi Meade

   Birth 1770 in North Castle, Westchester, New York, United States
   Death 27 Aug 1839 in Vermilion, Illinois, United States
Levi served in the war of 1812.

Their children:

Simeon Meade   1792 – 1866
Lewis Meade   1796 –
Mariah Meade   1799 – 1884
Nathaniel Meade   1800 – 1899
Amanda Meade   1800 – 1860
Sanford Meade   1800 – 1842
Louisa Meade   1805 –
Sarah Ann Meade   1806 –

GENERATION SEVEN

Abner Mead (1750-1810) and Mercy Hazen (1747-1819)

    x. JOHN, b. 1785, d. at Carmel, 23 Feb. 1822; m. 11 Jan. 1806, BETSEY WARR-
          BURN, b. 5 Feb. 1786, d. at Carmel, 3 May 1837. Five children.
    xi. JOSHUA, m. NANCY HOPKINS. Res. at La Porte, Ind.
    xii. NAOMA, d. aged 17.

123. MERCY[b] HAZEN (*Caleb[4], John[3], Thomas[2], Edward[1]*), born at Carmel, N. Y., about 1747; married ABNER MEAD, son of Amos Mead.

They removed from Putnam County to Roxbury, Delaware County, N. Y.,
perhaps about 1810, but it is said that they died at Middletown, Delaware
County. Not even approximate dates can be obtained from grandchildren.
It is said the Mead family had come from Connecticut to Frederickstown,
Dutchess County, about 1740.

Children (*Mead*):

    i. SARAH[c], b. at Kent, N. Y., 6 May 1770, d. at Clarks Green, Lackawanna
          Co., Pa., 6 May 1846; m. at Roxbury, N. Y., 1791, DAVID WHITE, b. at
          Kent, 9 Nov. 1769, d. at Wilsons Ferry, Pa., 25 May 1837, son of John
          and Margaret (Ogden) White. Nine children.
    ii. AMOS, d. in Fulton Co., Ohio; m. at Roxbury, N. Y., ELIZABETH GARRISON,
          daughter of David Garrison.
    iii. RUTH, m. JOSEPH NORTHROP, b. in Conn., 1770, d. at Margaretville, N. Y.,
          25 Sept. 1857, but near New Kingston, son of Solomon Northrop. Two
          children. He m. (2) Abigail Older, b. 1777, d. 1839.
    iv. DAVID, b. [11 June 1776], d. at Roxbury, N. Y., 30 Nov. 1844; m. there,
          ELIZABETH BALLARD, d. 30 June 1858 in her 78th year [g. s., Roxbury],
          daughter of Peleg and Martha (Haynes) Ballard. Seven children.
    v. CALEB, b. 17 Sept. 1779, d. in Fulton Co., Ohio, 14 July 1852; m. at Rox-
          bury, N. Y., MARY MORSE, b. in N. Y., Jan. 1780, d. in Fulton Co., Ohio,
          4 Apr. 1854, daughter of Joseph and Irena (Haynes) Morse. Ten
          children.
    vi. JAMES, b. 21 Dec. 1781, d. at Roxbury, N. Y., 17 May 1856; m. there,
          3 Feb. 1802, JERUSHA CRAFT, b. at Roxbury, 16 Mar. 1785, d. there 11
          July 1865, daughter of Jacob and Effie (Mabey) Craft. Thirteen children.
    vii. MARTHA, b. 1784, d. at Middletown, Delaware Co., N. Y., 3 Aug. 1860, but
          at Vega; m. JOHN MORSE, d. at Middletown, 15 July 1864, aged 88, but
          at Vega, son of Joseph and Irena (Haynes) Morse. Twelve children.
    viii. ELI, b. [3 May 1791], d. at Roxbury, N. Y., 27 Nov. 1842 [g. s. at Vega];
          m. JUDA JENKINS, b. 8 Apr. 1796, d. at Jewett, Greene Co., N. Y., 27 Nov.
          1880, daughter of Nathaniel Jenkins. Ten children.
    ix. ELEAZAR, b. 1793, d. at Clarks Green, Lackawanna Co., Pa.; m. at Roxbury,
          N. Y., ELIZABETH PARKER, b. 1799, d. at Clarks Green, daughter of Elijah
          Parker. Seven children.

124. (COL.) CALEB[b] HAZEN (*Caleb[4], John[3], Thomas[2], Edward[1]*), born
at Carmel, N. Y., 7 Nov. 1749, died there 31 Mar. 1806, aged 56 [gravestone,
Gilead Cemetery]; married RUTH WRIGHT, born 11 Nov. 1747, died at Carmel, 18 Dec. 1828, aged 77 [gravestone],* daughter of William Wright of
Scotland.

---

* The discrepancy in age is apparent. The birth record, like others in this family, is from a copy
of the lost original family record made by her grandson, Enos' Hazen.

Birth 24 Feb 1750 in Greenwich, Fairfield, Connecticut, United States

Death 1 June 1810 in Greenwich, Fairfield Co, CT

Children:

Sarah Mead - 1770 – 1846
Ruth Mead- 1774 – 1803
David Mead - 1776 – 1844
Caleb Mead - 1779 – 1852
James Mead - 1781 – 1856
Martha Mead - 784 – 1860
Amos Mead - 1786 – 1855
Eli B Mead - 1791 – 1842
Eleazor Mead - 1793 – 1865
Levi Mead - 1796 – 1871

FINDAGRAVE BIO

Birth: Feb. 22, 1750
Greenwich
Fairfield County
Connecticut, USA
Death: Jun. 1, 1810
Greenwich
Fairfield County
Connecticut, USA

Married Mercy Hazen 1770
childrn
Sarah 1770-1846
Amos 1772
Ruth 1774-1786
David 1776-1844
Caleb 1779-1852
James M 1781-1856

Martha 1784-1860
Eli 1791-1842
Eleazar 1793-1865
Levi 1798-1871
Might be buried in Old Cemetery area at Greenwich.

Family links:
 Parents:
  Silas Mead (1720 - 1817)
  Mary Mead Mead (1724 - 1787)

Spouse:
 Mercy Hazen Mead (1747 - 1810)*

Children:
 David Mead (1776 - 1844)*
 Eli Mead (1791 - 1842)*

Siblings:
 Silas Mead (1748 - 1813)*
 Abner Mead (1750 - 1810)
 Aaron Mead (1751 - 1818)*
 Alice Mead (1755 - 1776)*
 Mary Mead (1757 - 1761)*
 Calvin Mead (1760 - 1847)*
 Mary Mead Mead (1762 - 1837)*

GENERATION EIGHT

Silas Mead (1720-1807) and Mary Mead (1724-1787)

FIND A GRAVE BIO

Birth: May 21, 1720
Greenwich
Fairfield County
Connecticut, USA

Death: Oct. 13, 1817
Greenwich
Fairfield County
Connecticut, USA

Married Mary August 7, 1745 Greenwich, Connecticut
children
Silas 1748-1813
Abner 1750-1810
Alice 1755-1776
Mary 1757-1761
Calvin 1760-1847
Mary 1762-1837
Burial in Old North Greenwich Cemetery area.

MARY MEAD

FINDAGRAVE BIO

Birth: 1724
Greenwich
Fairfield County
Connecticut, USA
Death: Oct. 16, 1787
Greenwich
Fairfield County
Connecticut, USA

Father Benjamin Mead (1701 - 1783)
Mother Rachel Brown Mead (1690 - _____)
Married Silas Mead August 7, 1745 Greenwich, Connecticut
Burial in Old North Greenwich Cemetery area.

Family links:
 Spouse:
  Silas Mead (1720 - 1817)

 Children:
  Silas Mead (1748 - 1813)*
  Abner Mead (1750 - 1810)*
  Aaron Mead (1751 - 1818)*
  Alice Mead (1755 - 1776)*
  Mary Mead (1757 - 1761)*
  Calvin Mead (1760 - 1847)*
  Mary Mead Mead (1762 - 1837)*

GENERATION NINE

Ebenezer Mead (1692-1775) and Hannah Brown Mead (1691-1746)

[85] EBENEZER MEAD, JR.

EBENEZER MEAD, JR. was born in 1692 in Horseneck, a son of Ebenezer and Sarah (Knapp) Mead [#68]. Ebenezer, Jr., married **HANNAH BROWN**, born in 1698 in Rye, daughter of Peter and Martha (Disbrow) Brown, Jr. [#80]. Ebenezer, Jr., was a justice of the peace in Greenwich from 1733 to 1758, and was selected Greenwich's deputy to the Connecticut General Court in 1733, 1734, 1737 and 1738. He was a member of the town's Train Band, commissioned a lieutenant May 9, 1728, and a captain May 11, 1738. Ebenezer, who died in 1775, and Hannah (Brown) Mead, Jr., who died in 1783, had 11 children, including a son, Jonas [#91].

FIND A GRAVE BIOGRAPHY

Birth: Oct. 25, 1692
Greenwich
Fairfield County
Connecticut, USA
Death: Mar. 3, 1775
Greenwich
Fairfield County
Connecticut, USA

Father Ebenezer Mead 1663-1728
Mother Sarah Knapp 1670-1728
Married Hannah December 12, 1717 Stamford, Connecticut

children

Ebenezer 1718-1758
Silas 1720-1817
Abraham 1721-1743
Jonas 1723-1783
Solomon 1726-1812
Deliverance 1728-1785
Amos 1730-1807
Edmund 1732-1755

Hannah 1734-1757
Jared 1738-1832
Abraham 1731-1827
Jabez 1737-1766

Family links:
 Parents:
  Ebenezer Mead (1663 - 1728)
  Sarah Knapp Mead (1670 - 1746)

 Spouse:
  Hannah Brown Mead (1691 - 1746)

HANNAH BROWN REED

Birth: 1691
Rye
Westchester County
New York, USA
Death: Nov. 19, 1746
Greenwich
Fairfield County
Connecticut, USA

Married Ebenezer Decem,ber 12, 1717 Stamford, Connecticut

GENERATION TEN

 Ebenezer Mead 1663-1728 and Sarah Knapp 1670-1728

This is Ebenezer's tavern 1696

OLD TAVERN. EBENEZER MEAD LANDLORD IN 1698

FIND A GRAVE BIO

Birth: 1663
Greenwich
Fairfield County
Connecticut, USA
Death: 1728
Greenwich
Fairfield County
Connecticut, USA

Family links:

 Parents:
 John Mead (1634 - 1699)
 Hannah Brown Mead (1634 - 1700)
 Spouse:
 Sarah Knapp Mead (1670 - 1746)
 Children:
 Ebenezer Mead (1692 - 1775)*

Siblings:
Ebenezer Mead (1663 - 1728)
Hannah Mead Scofield (1664 - 1728)*
Benjamin Daniel Mead (1667 - 1746)*

SARAH KNAPP INFO

Birth: 1670
Stamford
Fairfield County
Connecticut, USA
Death: Nov. 19, 1746
Greenwich
Fairfield County
Connecticut, USA

Sarah and Ebenezer were the parents of:

Ebenezer/25 Oct 1692 m. Hannah Brown
Caleb/14 Jan 1694 m. Mary Holmes
Sarah/19 Oct 1695 (Mrs Jonathan Hobby)
Hannah/8 Nov 1698 (Mrs John Hobby)
Jabez/10 Jun 1700 m. Sarah Mills
David/10 Oct 1701 m. Sarah Close
Abigail/13 Sep 1703 (Mrs Isaac Holmes)
Susannah/28 Feb 1709 (Mrs Moses Husted)
John/1711
Jemima/12 Oct 1711 (Mrs Moses Knapp)
Alpheus/abt 1713

Family links:
 Parents:
  Caleb Knapp (1636 - 1675)
  Hannah Smith Lawrence (1641 - ____)

 Spouse:
  Ebenezer Mead (1663 - 1728)*

Children:
Ebenezer Mead (1692 - 1775)*

Sibling:
Hannah Knapp Palmer (1665 - _____)*
Sarah Knapp Mead (1670 - 1746)

GENERATION ELEVEN

John Mead (1634-1699) and Hannah Brown Mead (1634-1700)

Find a grave BIO

Birth: 1634, England
Death: Feb. 5, 1699
Greenwich
Fairfield County
Connecticut, USA

Family links:

Parents: William Mead (1600 - 1663)

Spouse: Hannah Brown Mead (1634 - 1700)*

Children:

Ebenezer Mead (1663 - 1728)*
Hannah Mead Scofield (1664 - 1728)*
Benjamin Daniel Mead (1667 - 1746)*

Sibling:

Joseph Mead (1630 - 1690)*
John Mead (1634 - 1699)

HANNAH BROWN INFO

Birth: Sep. 8, 1634
Death: Nov. 13, 1700
Greenwich
Fairfield County
Connecticut, USA

Hannah and John were the parents of:

John/15 Aug 1658 m. Ruth Hardy
Joseph/2 May 1660 m. Mary Smith
Hannah/abt 1661 (Mrs John Scofield)
Ebenezer/1663 m. Sarah Knapp
Jonathan/abt 1665 m. Martha Finch
David/abt 1665 m. Abigail Lyon
Benjamin/7 May 1667 m. Sarah Waterbury; 2) Rachel Brown
Nathaniel/abt 1669 m. Rachel ( )
Samuel/abt 1671 m. Hannah ( )
Abigail/abt 1673
Elizabeth/abt 1675
Mary/abt 1679

Family links:
 Parents:
  John Brown (1598 - 1636)
  Dorothy Brown Potter (_____ - 1673)

 Spouse:
  John Mead (1634 - 1699)

 Children:
  Ebenezer Mead (1663 - 1728)*
  Hannah Mead Scofield (1664 - 1728)*

     HANNAH BROWN'S FATHER IS FROM TRING, ENGLAND
born 1598

Birth: Apr., 1598
Tring, England
Death: Jun., 1636
Watertown
Middlesex County
Massachusetts, USA

Baptized Sawbridgeworth, Hertfordshire, 23 April 1598, son of
Edmund and Mary (Cramphorne) Brown.
Buried at Watertown 20 June 1636 "aged 36 years." Came from
Sawbridgeworth, Hertfordshire to Massachusetts Bay in 1632 on the
"Lyon" & settled in Watertown.
Married by 1634 Dorothy _____ (she was named in the birth record
of both daughters, and in the death record of her husband); probably
married (2) William Potter of Watertown, who moved in 1645 to
Stamford.
John Brown was brother of ABRAHAM BROWN of Watertown, of
Edmund Brown of Boston by 1634, and almost certainly of Hannah,
the wife of MATTHEW INES.

Family links:
 Spouse:
  Dorothy Brown Potter (____ - 1673)

Children:
 Hannah Brown Mead (1634 - 1700)*

GENERATION TWELVE

William Mead (1600 – 1663) and Martha Davis (1604-1657)

Birth: 1600
Lydd
Kent, England
Death: Sep. 19, 1663
Stamford
Fairfield County

Connecticut, USA

Family links:
 Children:
  Joseph Mead (1630 - 1690)*
  John Mead (1634 - 1699)*

Note: born in England, landed in Massachusetts in 1635; part of the family that founded Greenwich, Connecticut

Burial:
Tomac Burying Ground
Greenwich
Fairfield County
Connecticut, USA

MEAD

WILLIAM   JOSEPH
1600 — 1663   1630 — 1690
MARTHA   JOHN
1632   1634 — 1699
ALL BORN IN ENGLAND
LANDED IN MASS. IN 1635

THIS MONUMENT IS ERECTED BY
THE MEAD FAMILY AND FRIENDS
TO COMMEMORATE THE FOUNDING
OF THE TOWN OF GREENWICH
1640 — 1990

"*William Mead, born in England, about 1600, probably sailed from Lydd, County Kent, England, in the ship, Elizabeth, Captain Stagg, April 1635, for the Massachusetts Bay Colony; first settled in Wethersfield, Connecticut; removed to Stamford, Connecticut, in 1641, where he died about 1663. His wife died at Stamford, Sept. 19, 1657. Their children were: Joseph, Martha, and John. Joseph and John settled in the town of*

Greenwich. See "History & Genealogy of the Mead Family", Spencer Mead."

THE MEAD FAMILY

The Mead Family of Greenwich, Fairfield Co., Conn. was originally from England, and came to this country shortly after the Mayflower had landed its load of Pilgrims on the shores of Massachusetts. It has generally been the tradition in the family that two brothers came over; that one stopped at the Eastward, while the other came to Horse-Neck. That two brothers or possibly three, came over is very probable, as it would not be natural for one to come alone, could he find a relative to join him in his adventures. In the "History of Lexington, Mass." we find that Gabriel Mead was one of the earliest settlers of that place, as also David. The dates of their arrival, and of William of Horse-Neck (or rather Stamford) agree with one another, leading to the conclusion that all three were near relatives; furthermore the Coat-of -arms of both branches is identical, which is almost proof positive. It is not fully detemined from what part of England the Connecticut family came; but searches that have been made there seem to show a starting place somewhere near London, possibly Greenwich, Co. Kent.

The first record of any Mead in Fairfield Co. is the following in Stamford Town Records: "Dec. 7, 1641, William Mayd received from the town of Stamford, a homelot and 5 acres of land." This William was undoubtedly the ancestor of the Fairfield Co. Meads.

The tenacity with which the Meads have held their lands, and their love of home are by no means the least of their virtues, and it has been no uncommon thing for the same house and farm to have been handed down through five or six generations. Indeed some of the original purchases of land by the first families of Meads still remain in the possession of their descendants.

After a few years, they apparently joined a group of pioneer friends and neighbors and marches through the wilderness across Massachusetts to a new settlement called Wethersfield, CT. It was about 10 miles southeast of present-day Hartford on the banks of the Connecticut River. Wethersfield only proved to be a temporary home for the Meads. In 1641, they moved again, this time about 70 miles south and west to the small community of Stamford.

William's son John John Mead, the youngest child of colonial patriarch William Mead, was at best, very independent, headstrong, often at odds with authority in his early adult years. He had no profession, as such, but had started acquiring land ownership in the area at an early age. Disputes with others in the community were common and he seemed to have difficulty getting along with his Stamford neighbors. He had a number of run-ins with the community, its law enforcement officials and the church. After making so many people with angry he did spend time in prison for a while. Not long after this he and his brother Joseph went to Hempstead, Long Island.

William's daughter Martha had been charged for fornication for being pregnant with child some months before marriage.

GENERATION THIRTEEN

William Mead (1574-1649) and Elizabeth Colin (1578-1663)

Birth Mar 1574 in Wedmore, Somerset, England
Death 1649 in Somerset, England

GENERATION FOURTEEN

Henry Meade (1543 -1617) and Johanna Hooper (1547-1588) born in Wedmore, Somerset England, died same.

GENERATION FIFTEEN

Thomas Meade (1520-1596) and Joane Mathew Day (1522-1557)
      Birth 1520 in Wedmore, Somerset, England
      Death 1596 in Berdon, Essex, England

Joanne Day:
      Birth 1522 in Somerset, England
      Death 28 Aug 1557 in Berden, Essex, Engla

GENERATION SIXTEEN

Thomas Meade (1489-1557) and Joan Meade (1498-1548)

      Birth 1489 in Essex, England
      Death 1557 in Great Easton, Essex, England

Joan
      Birth 1522 in Somerset, England
      Death 28 Aug 1557 in Berden, Essex, Engla